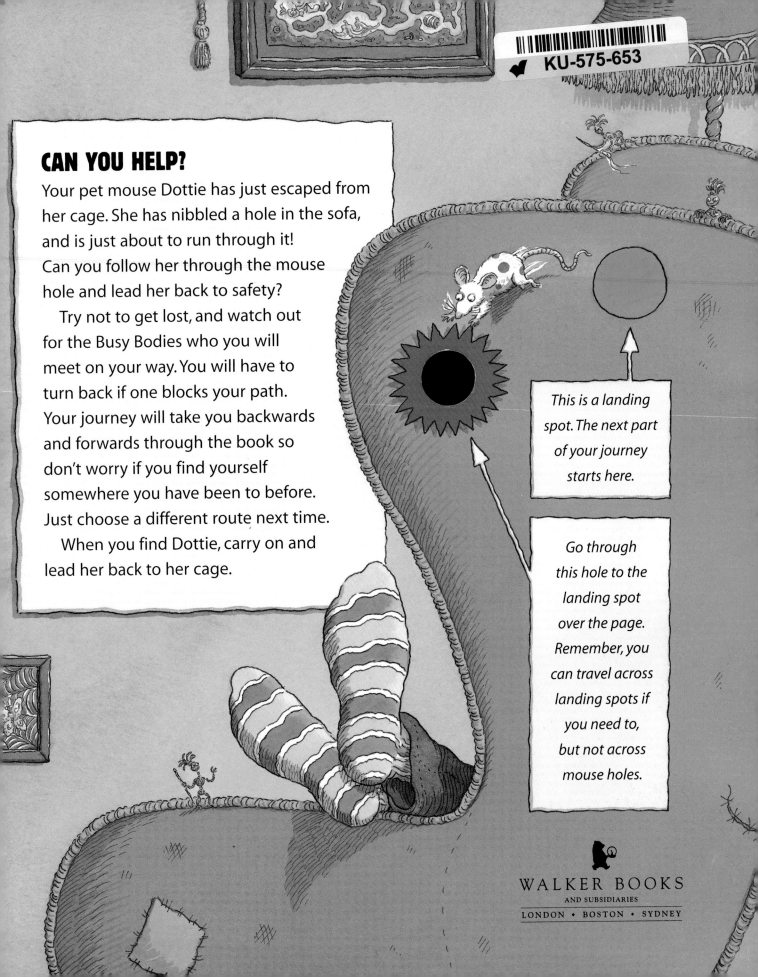

CAN YOU HELP?

Your pet mouse Dottie has just escaped from her cage. She has nibbled a hole in the sofa, and is just about to run through it! Can you follow her through the mouse hole and lead her back to safety?

Try not to get lost, and watch out for the Busy Bodies who you will meet on your way. You will have to turn back if one blocks your path. Your journey will take you backwards and forwards through the book so don't worry if you find yourself somewhere you have been to before. Just choose a different route next time.

When you find Dottie, carry on and lead her back to her cage.

This is a landing spot. The next part of your journey starts here.

Go through this hole to the landing spot over the page. Remember, you can travel across landing spots if you need to, but not across mouse holes.

WALKER BOOKS
AND SUBSIDIARIES

LONDON • BOSTON • SYDNEY

SOFA SPRINGS

You are deep inside the sofa! Busy Bodies are cleaning and mending. You must find a way along the springs and ropes to a mouse hole. Remember, if you meet a Busy Body, you'll have to turn back.

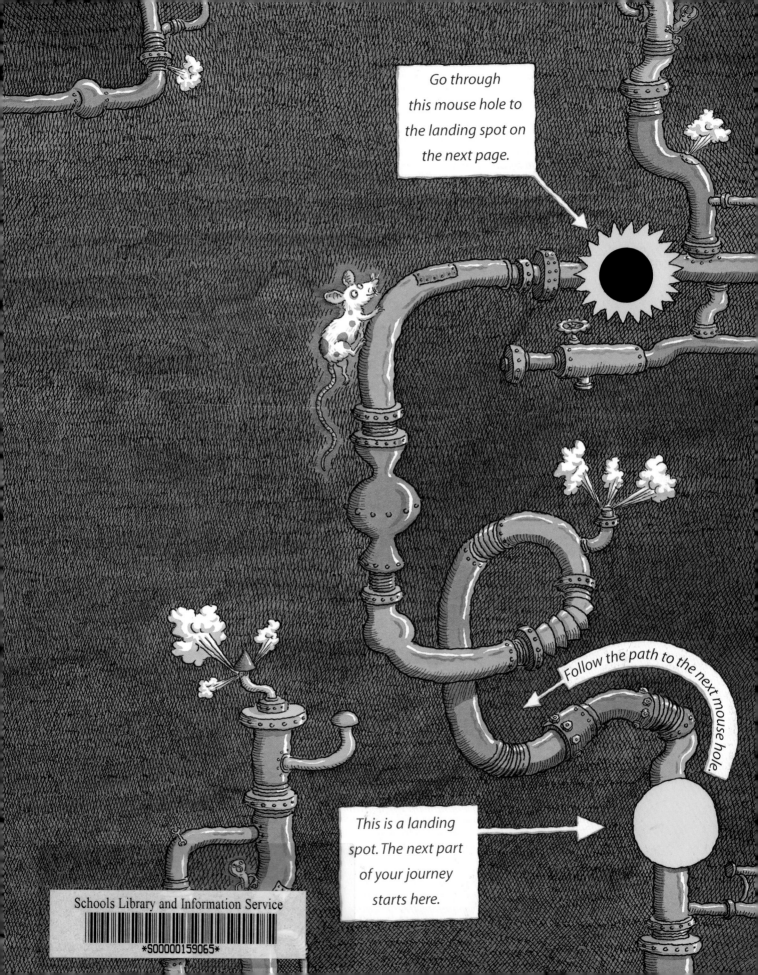

MOUSEMAZIA

ANNA NILSEN

ILLUSTRATED
DOM MANSELL

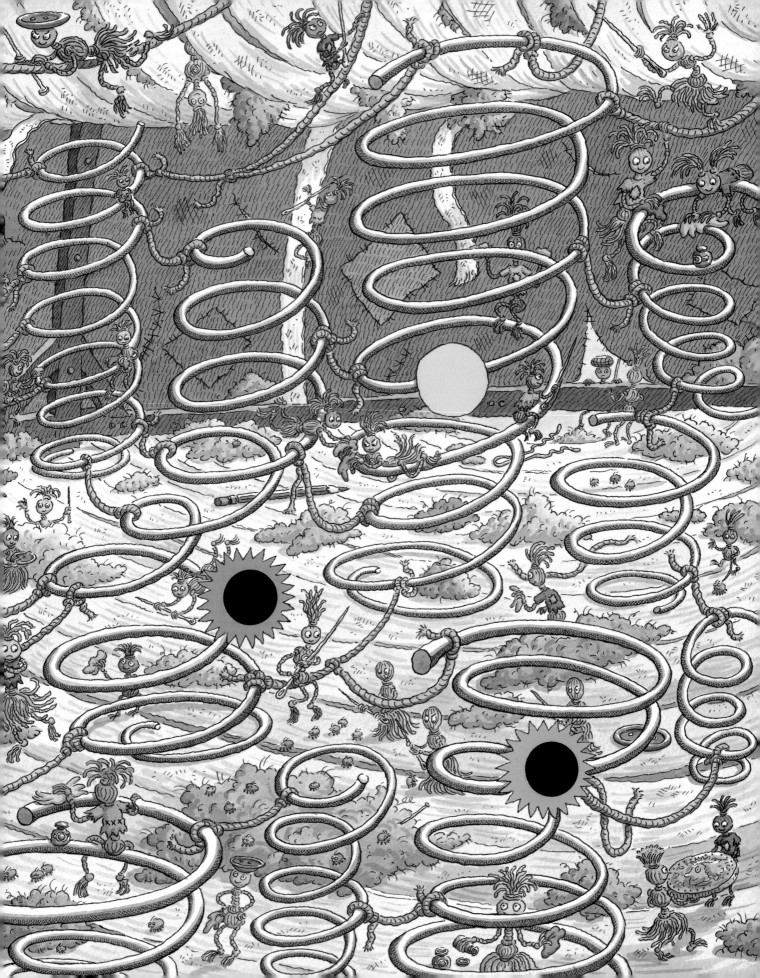

DREAM CUSHION

Dottie has nibbled her way up into a cushion. It's full of feathers and lots of Busy Bodies blocking your way! Find a path between the feathers to reach a mouse hole.

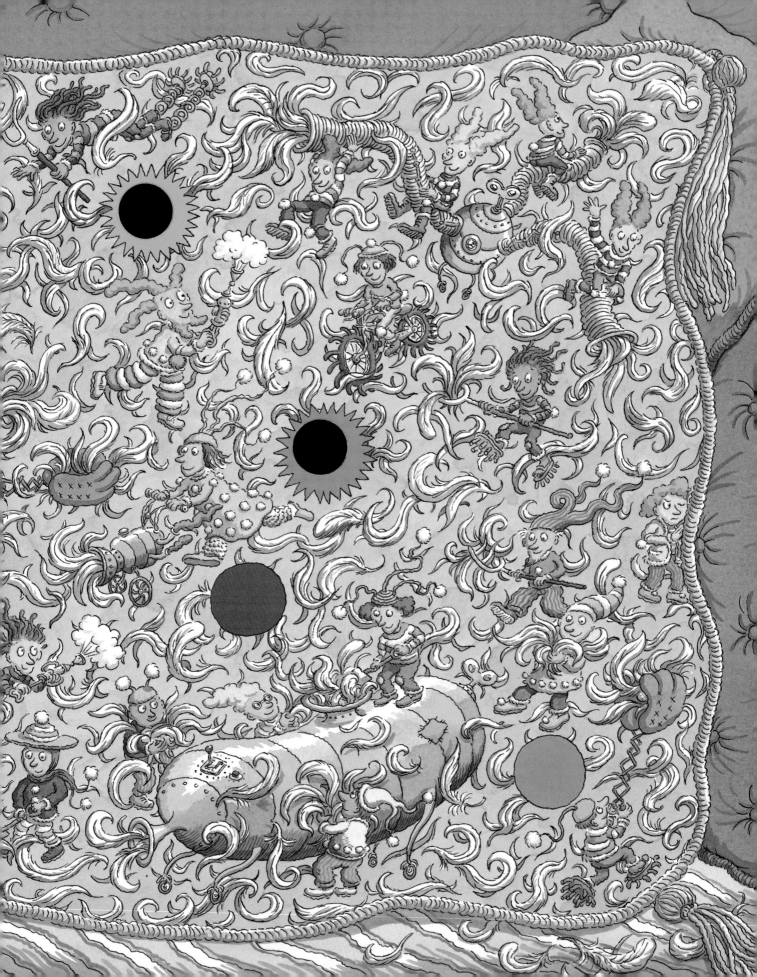

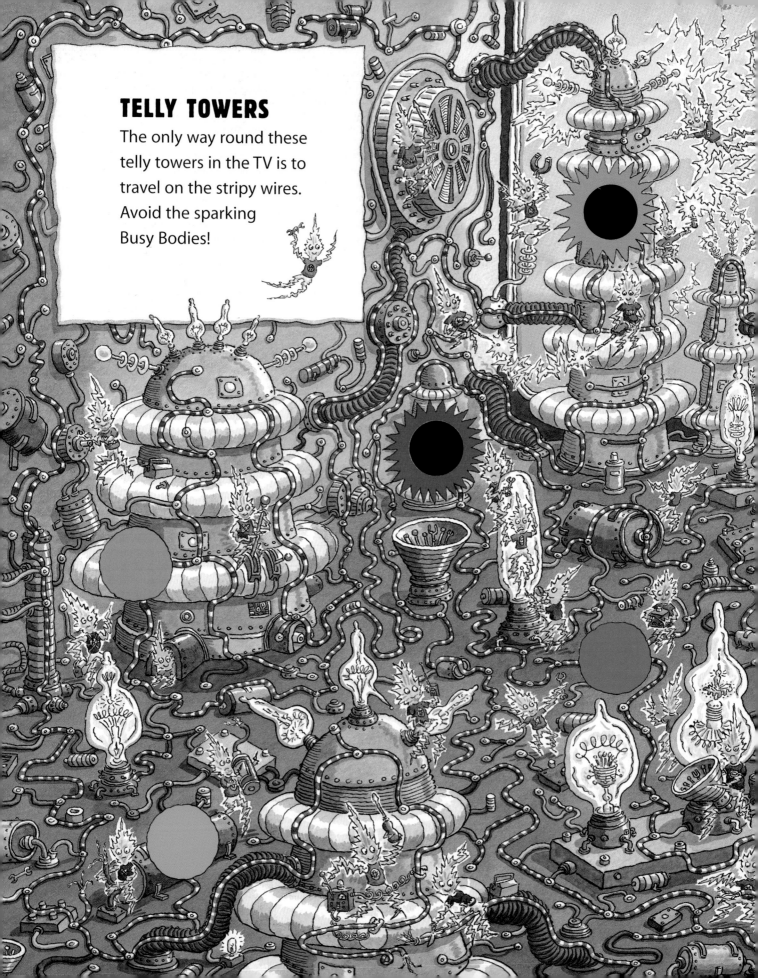

TELLY TOWERS

The only way round these telly towers in the TV is to travel on the stripy wires. Avoid the sparking Busy Bodies!

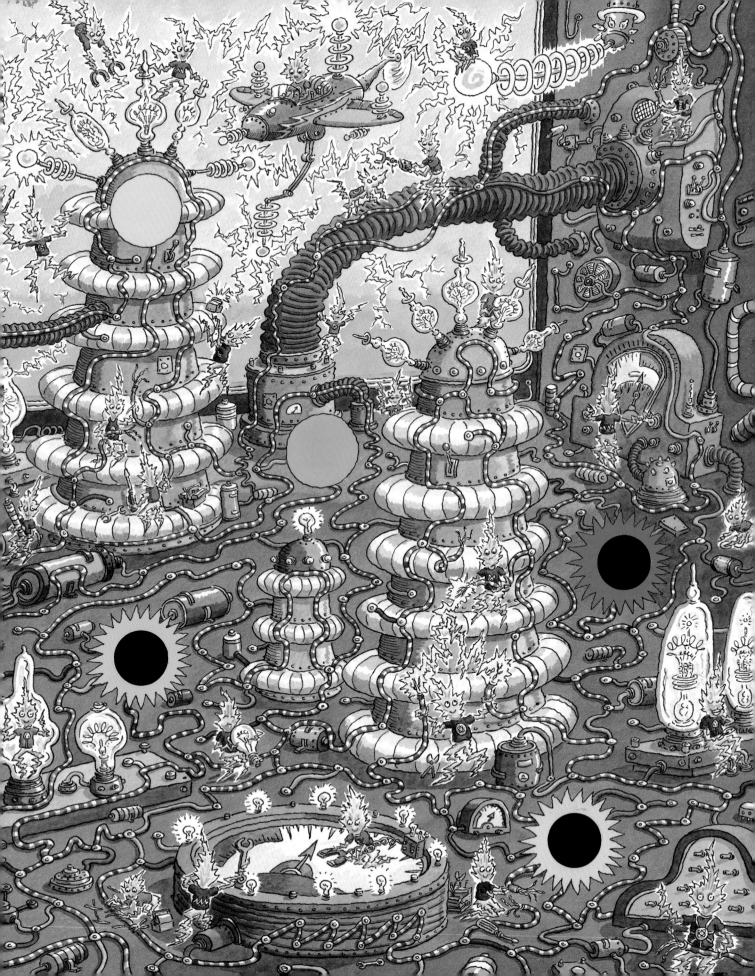

COG CITY

Now you are inside the clock! What a lot of wheels and cogs, all whirring and ticking! Travel along touching cog wheels and if you meet one of the Busy Body timekeepers, turn back at once!

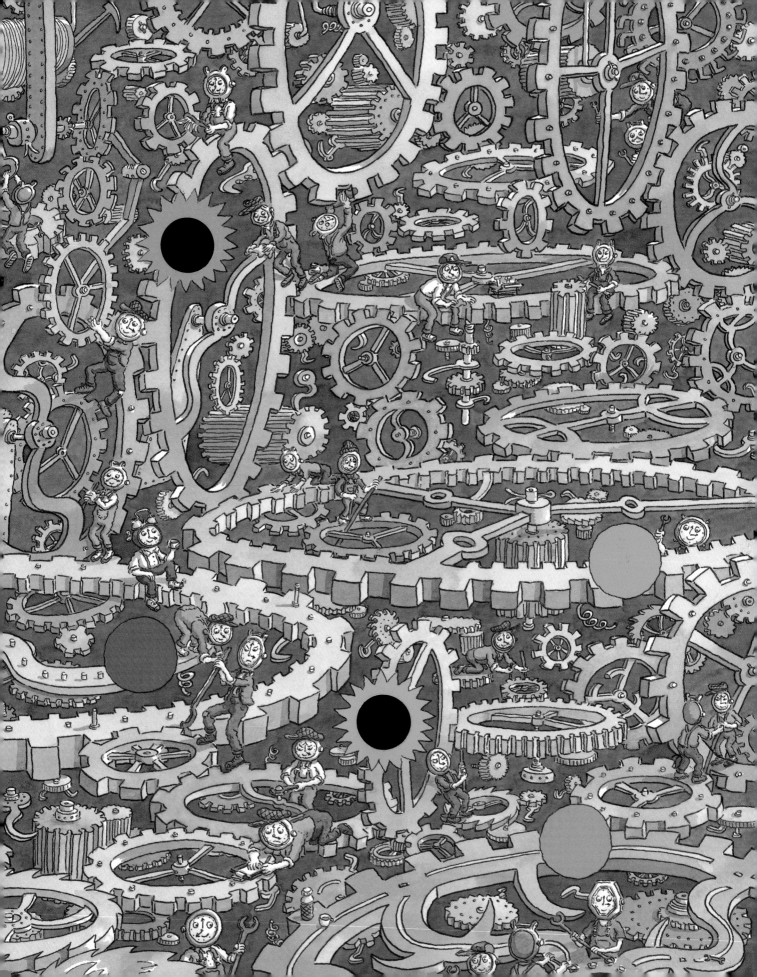

WHISTLING PIPES

Swishh! Shwoo! Where are you? Among the heating pipes! Follow the pipes to escape, avoiding the clouds of steam and the Busy Body spanners.

COBWEB CAVERN

Ugh! Webs and spiders everywhere! Look out for the Busy Bodies too. To get out, find an unblocked path along the webs. Good luck!

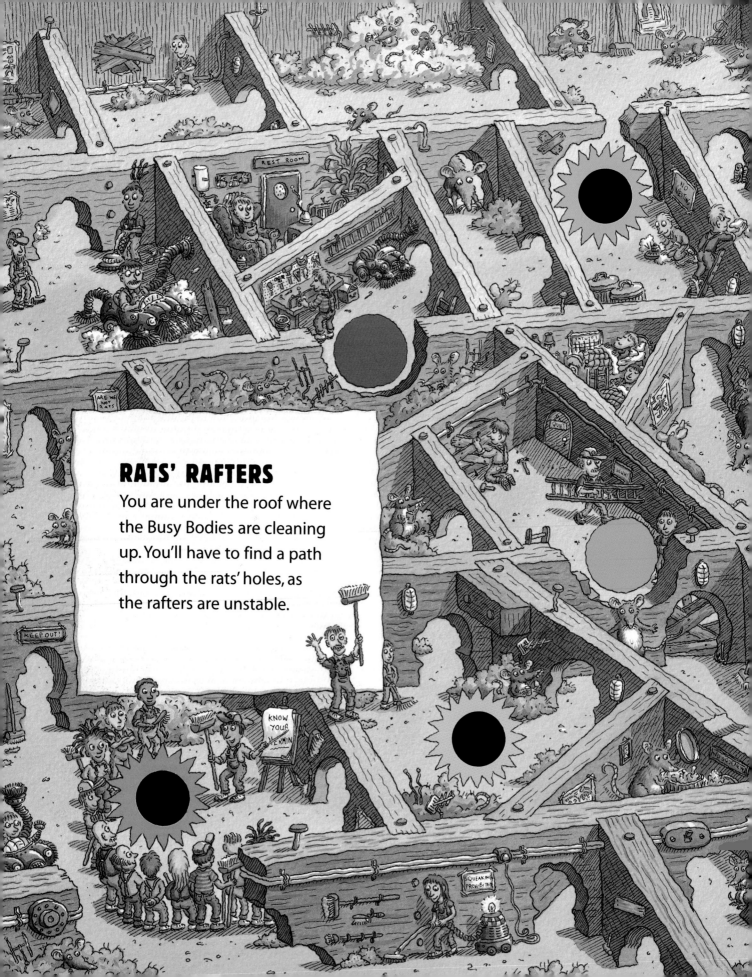

RATS' RAFTERS

You are under the roof where the Busy Bodies are cleaning up. You'll have to find a path through the rats' holes, as the rafters are unstable.

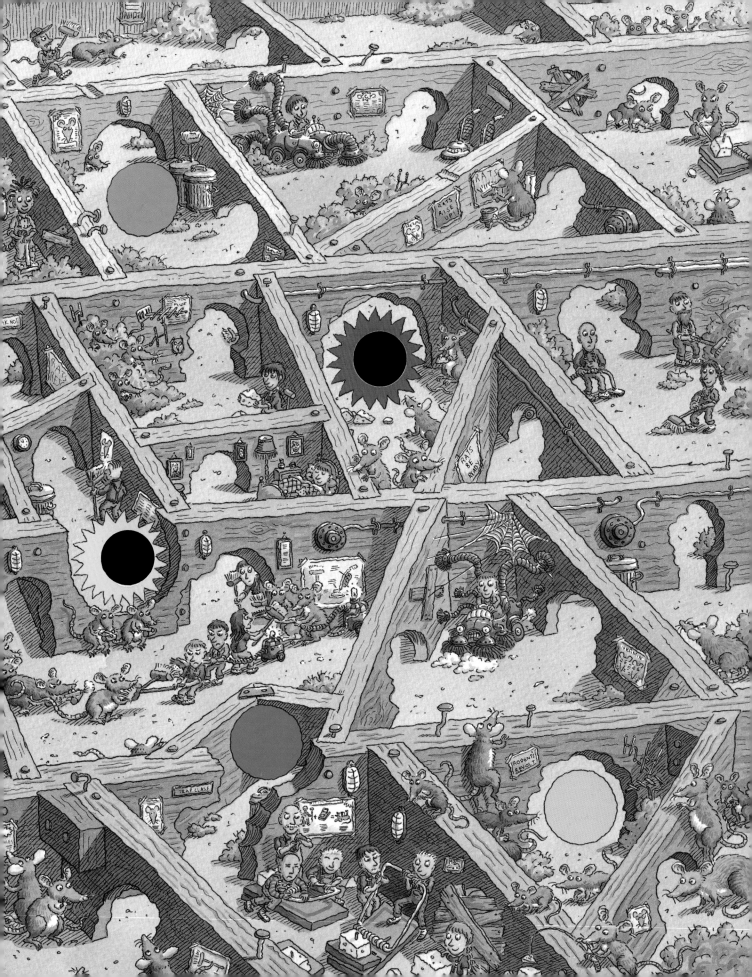

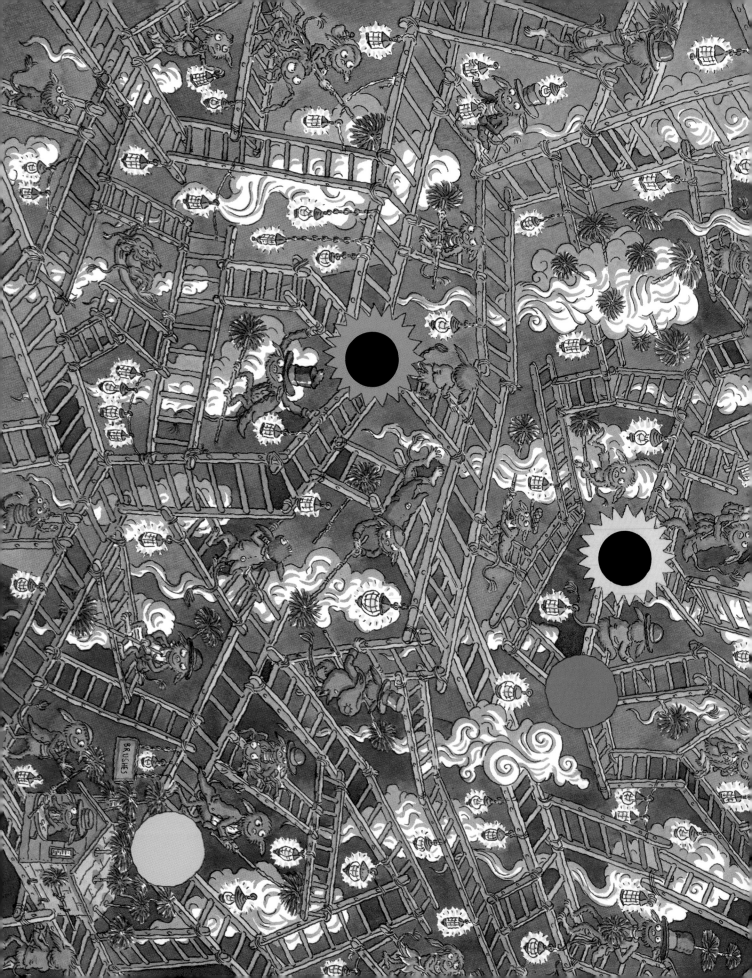

CHIMNEY STACK

Busy Body chimney sweeps are removing soot and grime in the darkness. If you meet one on a ladder, you must turn back. See if there's a path along the empty ladders. Take care not to fall!

ROOF

Here you are up in the sky! The roof tiles are slippery with moss and covered with Busy Body cleaners. Find a clear path across the tiles to get safely off this roof.

CLINGING IVY

How can you get to the ground again? The Busy Bodies are in the way – snipping off dead leaves, cleaning up snail trails and watering. Find a way down by following the stems up, down and around. Stay away from the slippery leaves!

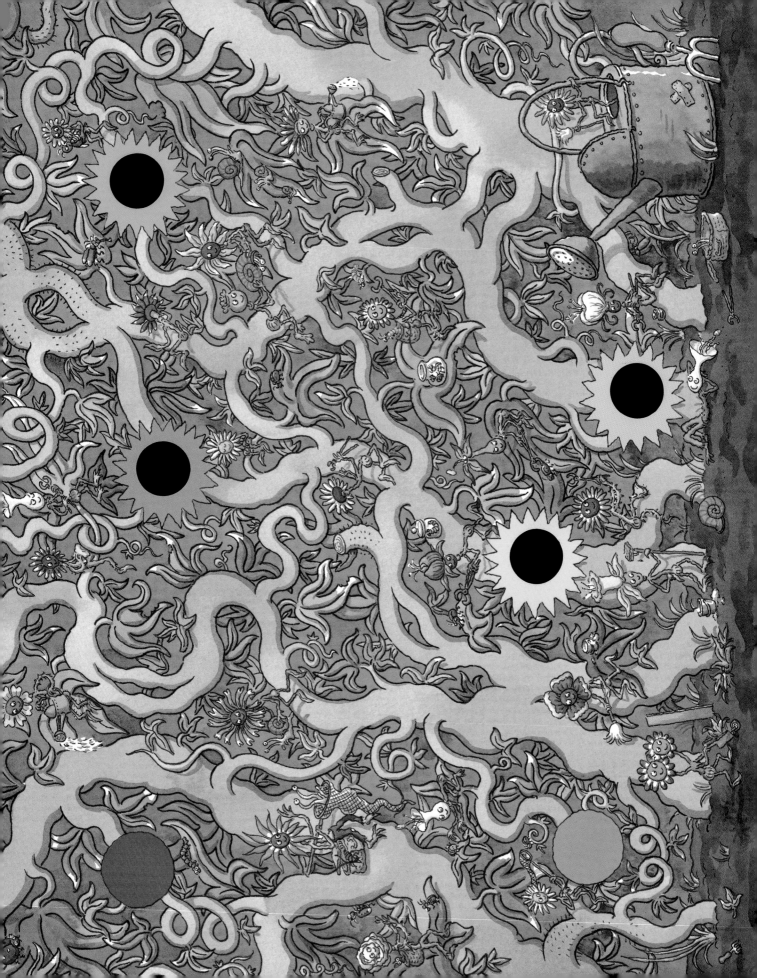

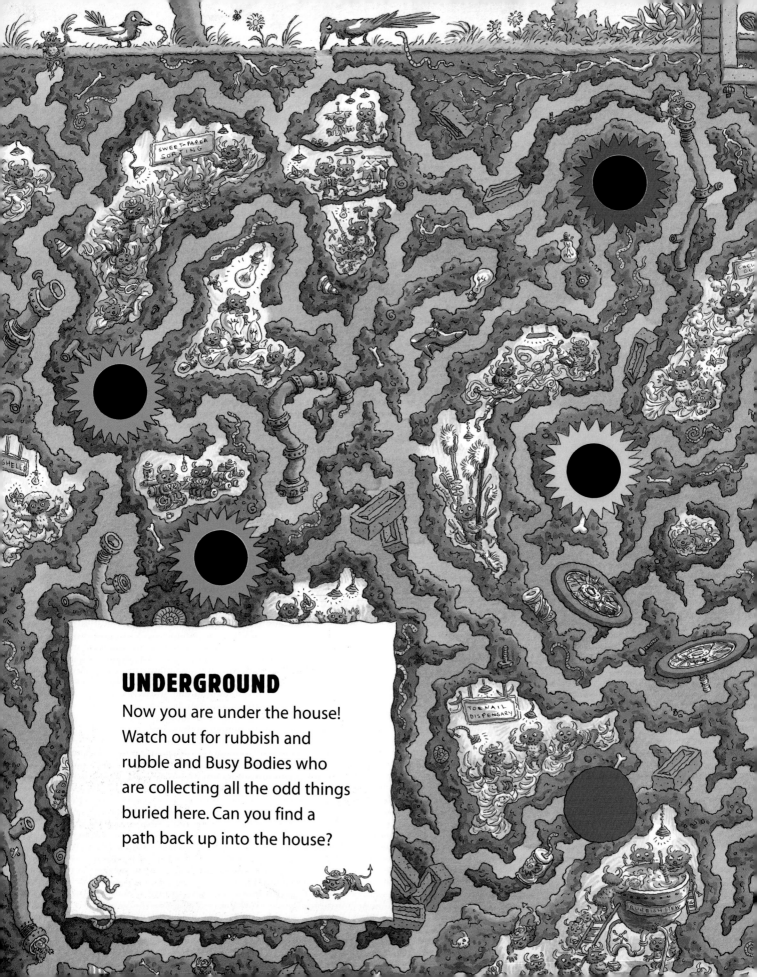

UNDERGROUND

Now you are under the house! Watch out for rubbish and rubble and Busy Bodies who are collecting all the odd things buried here. Can you find a path back up into the house?

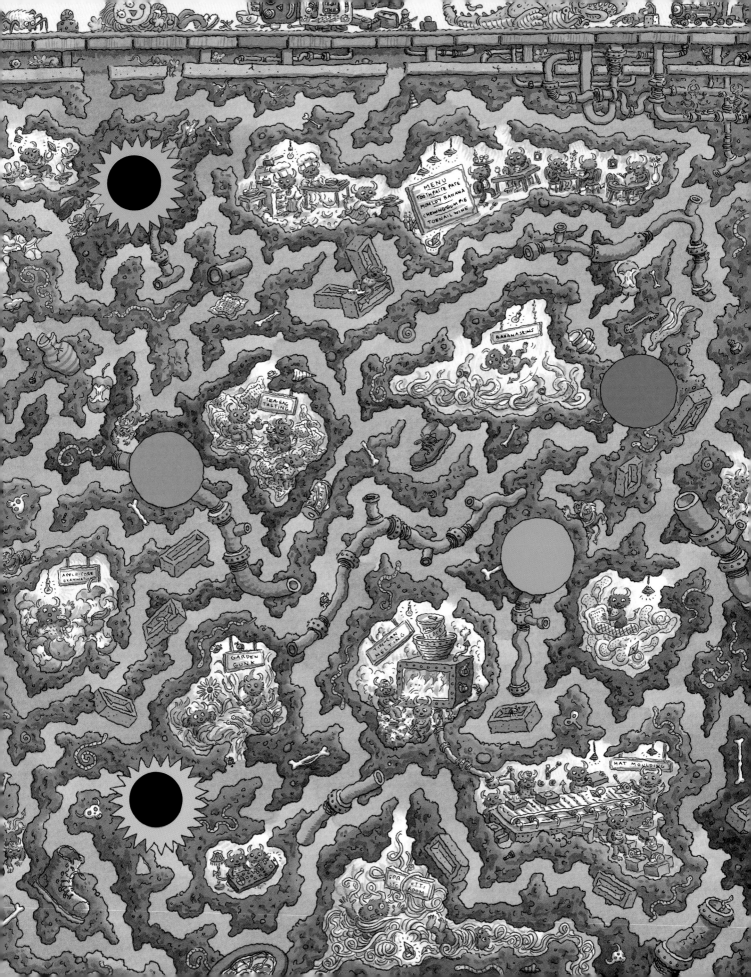

PLAYROOM

Well done! You have led Dottie back to her cage.

But wait! Dottie knocked over the jewellery box and ten rings have been lost. First find the ruby ring in this room, then trace a path from it to the dark hole in the floor. Go through the hole and find nine emerald rings under ground. Take them back to the jewellery box and your task is finally done!

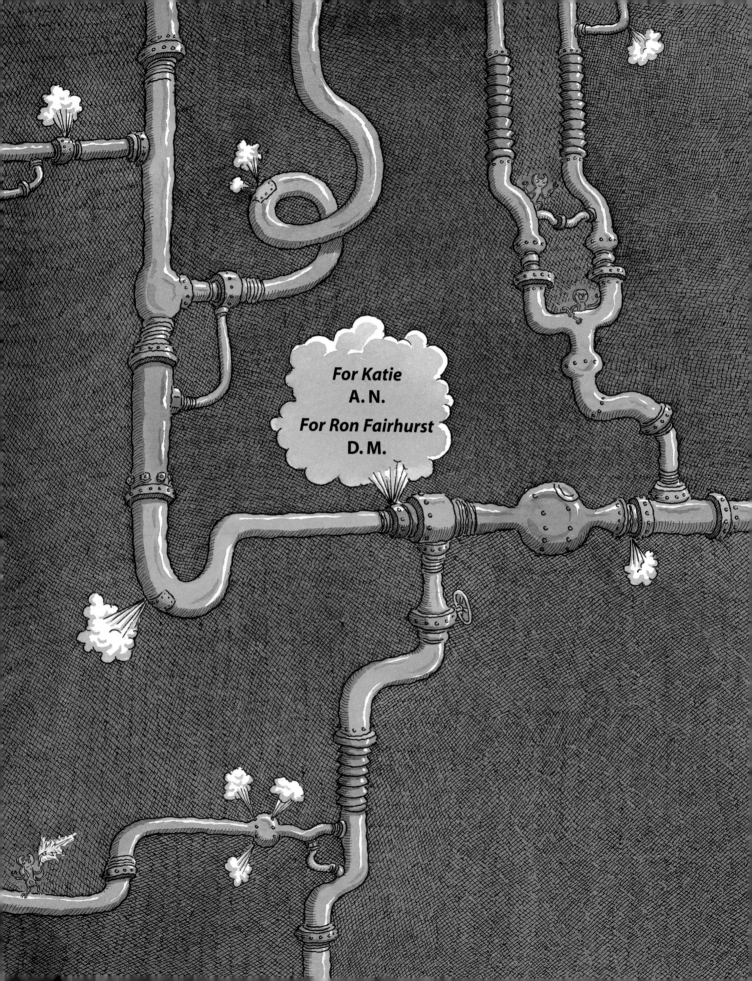

For Katie
A. N.

For Ron Fairhurst
D. M.